Spot the Difference

Seeds

Charlotte Guillain

Heinemann Library
Chicago, Illinois

Customer Service 888-454-2279
Visit our website at www.heinemannraintree.com

Designed by Joanna Hinton-Malivoire
Photo research by Erica Martin and Hannah Taylor
Printed and bound in China by South China Printing Co. Ltd.
12 11 10 09 08
10 9 8 7 6 5 4 3 2 1

Library of Congress Cataloging-in-Publication Data
Guillain, Charlotte.
    Seeds / Charlotte Guillain.
       p. cm. -- (Spot the difference)
    Includes index.
    ISBN-13: 978-1-4329-0946-8 (lib. bdg.-hardcover)
    ISBN-10: 1-4329-0946-0 (lib. bdg.-hardcover)
    ISBN-13: 978-1-4329-0953-6 (pbk.)
    ISBN-10: 1-4329-0953-3 (pbk.)
    1. Seeds--Juvenile literature. I. Title.
    QK661.G85 2008
    581.4'67--dc22

                          2007036312

Acknowledgements
The publishers would like to thank the following for permission to reproduce photographs: ©Alamy pp.**18**, **23a** (Christopher Griffin); ©Bjanka Kadic pp.**12**, **23c** (flowerphotos.com); ©Corbis pp.**5** (PBNJ Productions/PBNJ Productions), **10 right** (louds Hill Imaging Ltd); ©FLPA pp.**7**, **23b** (Inga Spence), **19** (John Watkins), **6** (Nigel Cattlin); ©Geoscience Features Picture Library p.**16** (Dr.B.Booth); ©Getty Images p.**15** (Science Faction); ©istockphoto.com pp.**4 bottom right** (Stan Rohrer), **4 top left** (CHEN PING-HUNG), **4 top right** (John Pitcher), **10 left** (ranplett), **4 bottom left** (Vladimir Ivanov); ©Nature picture library pp. **13**, **23d** (Jose B. Ruiz); ©Photolibrary pp.**11**, **22 left** (Botanica), **8**, **9**, **21**, (Animals Animals / Earth Scenes), **14**, **22 right** (Mark Bolton), **17** (Satoshi Kuribayashi); ©Science photo library p**20** (Larry Miller).

Cover photograph of coral bean seeds reproduced with permission of ©Photolibrary (Animals Animals / Earth Scenes). Back cover photograph of horse chestnut seeds reproduced with permission of ©Bjanka Kadic (flowerphotos.com).

Every effort has been made to contact copyright holders of any material reproduced in this book. Any omissions will be rectified in subsequent printings if notice is given to the publishers.

Contents

What Are Plants?

Plants are living things.
Plants live in many places.

Plants need air to grow.
Plants need water to grow.
Plants need sunlight to grow.

What Are Seeds?

flower

leaf

stem

roots

Plants have many parts.

Plants grow from seeds.

Different Seeds

These are sunflower seeds.
They are black.

These are coral bean seeds.
They are red.

seed

This is a strawberry.
It has small seeds.

seed

This is a coconut tree.
It has big seeds.

These are horse chestnut seeds.
They are smooth.

These are cranesbill seeds.
They are spiky.

Amazing Seeds

These are sycamore seeds.
They have wings to carry them.

These are dandelion seeds.
They have hairs to carry them.

This is a goosegrass seed.
It has hooks so animals can carry it.

This is a trillium seed.
It is small so insects can carry it.

These are beech seeds.
They float in water.

These are mistletoe seeds.
They stick to birds.

What Do Seeds Do?

Seeds travel to a new place.

seed

Seeds grow into
new plants.

Spot the Difference!

How many differences can you see?

Picture Glossary

 **float** to stay on top of water

 **seed** the part of the plant that can grow into a new plant

 **smooth** flat; does not have bumps

 **spiky** has sharp points

Index

Note to Parents and Teachers

Before reading
Show the children seeds of different colors. Talk to the children about how most plants grow from seeds. Explain that the seeds come from the flower of a plant. When they drop to the ground, they begin to grow and make a new plant.

After reading
Show the children some seeds we eat (e.g. peas, beans, cucumbers, strawberries, and corn). Show them fruit seeds that we do not eat (e.g. apples, melons, oranges, or peaches).